Jun. 15, 2011

WITHDRAWN

AMENDMENTS TO THE UNITED STATES CONSTITUTION
THE BILL OF RIGHTS

LIMITING FEDERAL POWERS

THE TENTH AMENDMENT

TAMRA ORR

rosen publishing's
rosen
central

New York

Published in 2011 by The Rosen Publishing Group, Inc.
29 East 21st Street, New York, NY 10010

Library of Congress Cataloging-in-Publication Data

Orr, Tamra.
The Tenth Amendment: limiting federal powers / Tamra Orr. — 1st ed.
    p. cm. — (Amendments to the United States Constitution : the Bill of Rights)
Includes bibliographical references and index.
ISBN 978-1-4488-1265-3 (library binding)
ISBN 978-1-4488-2311-6 (pbk.)
ISBN 978-1-4488-2320-8 (6-pack)
1. Federal government—United States—Juvenile literature. 2. States' rights (American politics—Juvenile literature. 3. United States. Constitution. 10th Amendment—Juvenile literature. I. Title.
KF4600.O77 2011
342.73'042—dc22

2010021852

Manufactured in the United States of America

CPSIA Compliance Information: Batch #W11YA: For further information, contact Rosen Publishing, New York, New York, at 1-800-237-9932.

On the cover: Left: As the Supreme Court hears arguments about the federal government's powers to prevent doctors from helping terminally ill patients end their lives, protesters outside the Supreme Court building express their disapproval of physician-assisted suicide. Center: A protester expresses anger over the health care reform bill. Right: A rally on Wall Street in New York City protests federal government bailouts of struggling financial institutions. The extent of the federal government's powers and how it raises and spends taxpayer money are issues that are often interpreted through the Tenth Amendment by Supreme Court justices.

CONTENTS

INTRODUCTION

U nderstanding President Barack Obama's one-thousand-plus page, trillion-dollar health care reform bill that was drafted in 2010 was enough to challenge most people. Its length, incredible complexity, and dense political jargon made it difficult reading. Many of its thousands of sentences were peppered with clauses like, "For the purpose of subparagraph 17(b) . . ." Whether or not they had actually read it, however, some people quickly spoke out against it—often with great confidence and at high volume.

Congress voted on the health care bill in March 2010, and it passed by a very slim margin of 219 to 212. Although it was often difficult to understand all of its points and subpoints, the bill's overall purpose was

The spirit and passion behind the original Boston Tea Party more than two hundred years ago was seen again in the Code Red rallies held across the country to protest the health care reform bill. At this march in Washington, hundreds of demonstrators came out to show their opposition to the new health care legislation.

relatively simple: it was designed to respond to the country's growing health care crisis by expanding Americans' health insurance coverage. How? The bill required all individuals to have insurance, either through an employer or through a private insurance company. What happens if a person chooses not to purchase insurance? Starting in 2014, he or she will have to pay a hefty annual penalty—one that will increase over time.

All of this may be vital to the health and well-being of American society and of great financial concern to the nation's businesses and heads of household. But what does the president's health care reform bill have to do with amendments to the U.S. Constitution? A number of people believe that Obama's health care bill was not only a policy mistake, but that the law is also unconstitutional. These critics believe that it violates the state and individual rights enshrined in the Constitution and is therefore illegal. These opponents strongly feel that the new health care law is in direct violation of the Tenth Amendment in particular. "I don't believe Congress has the legal or moral authority to force this mandate on its citizens," says John Ensign, Republican senator for Nevada (as quoted by FOX News in December 2009).

Senator Ensign and other like-minded people, including the members of the Tenth Amendment Center (also known as "Tenthers"), were concerned that Obama's new legislation stood in direct violation of the Tenth Amendment to the Constitution. They were so sure of it, in fact, that a number of state senators filed lawsuits against Congress protesting the bill's passage. Kelly Shackelford, chief counsel of the conservative Liberty Legal Institute, states in an interview with FOX News that "there are a lot of states that are concerned that this [bill] violated the Tenth Amendment, and they are weighing their options."

The Tenth Amendment is one of the least understood—and therefore the most debated—amendments in the Bill of Rights, which are the first ten amendments to the Constitution. Unlike the first eight, both the Ninth and Tenth amendments do not spell out specific, concrete rights that are easy to identify and name. These two amendments are much more abstract and vague in their wording. This has caused a great deal of trouble over the centuries, ever since they were first ratified in the late eighteenth century.

The Tenth Amendment states, "The powers not delegated to the United States by the Constitution, not prohibited by it to the States, are reserved for the States respectively, or to the people." What does this mean? It states a simple truth: There are powers that belong to the federal government, but those that do not belong to the federal government belong to the individual states and the people who live in them. The amendment was a strong reminder to all citizens that while the government was powerful and essential, it was not all-powerful. Unlike the British Empire it had recently broken away from, the still young United States of America would not be characterized by tyranny or dictatorship.

The Tenth Amendment emphasized that states and their residents had important rights that could not be taken away from them by the federal government. This was a constitutional assurance that the people of this newly formed nation required. After all, individual rights and self-rule were what the American colonists had been battling Britain for both before and during the American Revolution. These were ideals that many Americans had sacrificed their safety, security, homes, and even lives to gain. They weren't about to let a government of their own choosing take away what had been so hard fought and dearly won.

CHAPTER ONE
LIMITING FEDERAL POWER

I magine how the Founding Fathers and former colonists must have felt when they finally achieved the freedom they had fought so hard for. For all of their lives, they had been under the control of England, its Parliament, and its king. They had to follow rules they disagreed with and obey decisions and decrees they had no part in making. They were told how to conduct their businesses, and they were taxed heavily. Yet they did not have the right to speak out in protest or have their views represented in Parliament. Many American colonists felt trapped and oppressed, relentlessly squeezed by a tyrannical government that refused to listen to their wants and needs.

The colonists finally declared independence and eventually drove the British Army from what had become the United States of America. They were excited and eager to start their new lives as free and self-governing American citizens. Their exhilaration over this newfound liberty and independence was understandable—but it was also brief. With freedom comes unexpected responsibility. Suddenly, the citizens and their appointed leaders had to address, debate, and resolve serious, complicated questions about governing. Creating a new government that would rule wisely and fairly was much harder than criticizing and rebelling against an existing government. It was difficult to decide how to create a government that would lead without tyrannizing, support the states and its citizens without controlling, and provide structure to society without dominating it.

Finding a Balance

During the years when the American Revolution raged, the thirteen original states (the former colonies) remained largely united because they all shared the same goal: independence from Britain. Once they had gained that, however, they found themselves struggling with a whole new set of problems. One of the primary ones was how to rule their new land. They already knew they did not want to replicate the victimization they experienced when they were British colonies. In the newly independent United States, there was to be no king, no royal family, and no lack of freedom in religion or speech. The states and their citizens knew what they didn't want in a new government. But what exactly did they want? What powers and structure did they want the federal government to have?

In the post-Revolutionary War years, debates and discussions led to a few important decisions. Americans wanted their new nation to be a republic, or a government that was based on the will and consent of the people. They wanted a leader that would be elected on his or her merits and abilities and not because of royal heritage, an influential family, wealth, or powerful connections. They wanted a government that would give the nation and society structure, but one that wouldn't have the power to control their personal and private lives. Finding this balance was not easily achieved.

A First Attempt

The first document that attempted to outline the powers and structure of the new country's federal government was the Articles of Confederation. Drafted in 1777, it was ratified four years later. The Articles of Confederation established a permanent national congress made up of from between two and seven delegates each of the thirteen states.

Congress had a few select powers: It could declare war or peace, handle foreign relations, and keep an army and navy (though it couldn't draft soldiers or supply them). It could make laws but had no power to enforce them. There was no executive branch (a president and cabinet offices) or judicial branch (the Supreme Court and other federal courts) under the Articles of Confederation.

Independence Hall in Philadelphia was the site of countless debates during the drafting of the Constitution. Could the men who worked so hard on this document have imagined that some of the same issues would still be fought over more than two hundred years later?

Regarding what powers the federal government had as compared to states' rights, Article II of the document declared that "each state retains its sovereignty, freedom, and independence, and every power, jurisdiction, and right, which is not by this Confederacy expressly

delegated to the United States, in Congress assembled." This meant that any power not explicitly reserved for the federal government in the Articles of Confederation automatically belonged to the states. The federal government—which consisted only of Congress at this point—had very few powers granted to it. So the states retained many rights and enormous governing power under the Articles of Confederation.

Strengthening a Rope of Sand

For a short time, it appeared that the Articles of Confederation were all the country needed. As time went on, however, the weak federal government proved incapable of uniting an expanding nation or governing it effectively. Indeed, General George Washington, the future first president of the United States, recognized early on that a weak federal government would prove to be a "rope of sand." He meant that it was an inadequate, easily broken tie to bind the independent states together.

It soon became apparent that the federal government had too little power to be effective under the Articles of Confederation. For example, there was no executive or judicial branch of government (a president or Supreme Court) and no power to collect taxes, regulate commerce between the states, or raise and fund an army. The clamor for changes to the Articles of Confederation grew. Clearly, something better was needed, and the federal government needed to be strengthened.

During the summer of 1787, fifty-five delegates from the thirteen states met in Philadelphia, Pennsylvania. They gathered to determine how to create a document that provided for a stronger, more effective federal government, yet one that didn't sacrifice state or individual rights. It took almost four months for thirty-nine of the fifty-five delegates to sign the final draft of the Constitution. Nine of the thirteen states would have to ratify the document for it to go into effect.

The Federalist Papers

During the two years that the Constitution was being drafted and debated, politicians did not have many ways to reach the American people and share their opinions and ideas. In the late eighteenth century, there was only one means of relatively fast mass communication: letters to the editors of city newspapers.

In the six months before the Constitution's ratification, a series of eighty-five letters were published in a number of New York newspapers. They were primarily written by the Federalists Alexander Hamilton, James Madison, and John Jay. Yet readers did not know the true identities of the writers; the letters were written under the pen name **Publius**. Each one of the letters and essays discussed in detail the many reasons why the new Constitution should be ratified.

At the same time, a number of other letters were written in response by Anti-Federalist authors who used pen names such as Cato, Centinel, Federal Farmer, and Brutus. These were also published in New York newspapers, and they detailed the reasons why the Constitution should be thoroughly questioned, analyzed, and amended before ratification.

Readers loved reading each new letter. It was like watching a battle being played out on paper, with words and wit as weapons. With each argument and rebuttal that was printed, the national debate took shape and was hashed out. In the process, the American public was educated in the minute details of the philosophy of governance and constitutional law, allowing them to make their own informed conclusions about the proper shape their government should assume and the direction the country should take.

Alexander Hamilton was a prominent Federalist and one of the leading anonymous authors of the Federalist Papers.

On June 21, 1788, New Hampshire became the ninth state to ratify the Constitution. Eight months later, it went into effect. By 1790, all thirteen of the original states had ratified the U.S. Constitution.

This remarkable document consisted of two parts: the introduction, often referred to as the Preamble, and the body, composed of seven sections called Articles. These Articles describe legislative power, executive power, judicial power, states' powers and limits, the amendment process, federal power, and the ratification process.

Second Thoughts: Amending the New Constitution

After all the hard work and passionate debate that went into its drafting and ratification, it seems like the Constitution should have been relatively easy for everyone to accept by the end of the process. Just the opposite was true, however. Even before it had been approved, some delegates were already complaining and asking for changes to be made to it. Many people felt that, while the Constitution was a good start, it did not provide enough protection for average citizens against potential government abuse.

The original copies of the Declaration of Independence, the Constitution, and the Bill of Rights are kept at the National Archives in Washington, D.C. They are under the watchful eyes of honor guards at all times.

The anxiety was easy to understand. After all they had lived through under tyrannical British rule, the people in this new nation insisted upon a better government than what they had during the colonial era. While they had been waiting for a national constitution, the states had

already formed individual declarations that included the freedom of speech, freedom of the press, and the right to a trial by a jury for their citizens. State delegates wanted to see a similar bill of rights built into the Constitution.

As a result, a series of ten constitutional amendments, known collectively as the Bill of Rights, was proposed in 1789 and ratified in 1791. These amendments were created to address questions or rights missing or requiring clarification in the original Constitution. In the years since the Bill of Rights was ratified, another seventeen amendments to the Constitution have been passed into law. These later amendments tackle issues such as the abolition of slavery, voting rights for African Americans and women, the national voting age, and presidential term limits.

The fierce debates and disagreements over the Constitution and the Bill of Rights among delegates to the Constitutional Convention exposed a major philosophical divide in America. On one side were those who felt that the federal government should serve as a strong central command with a great deal of power. This centralized power would help bind the states together and prevent chaos. Without a strong central government, it was argued, the United States would actually be a disunited collection of independent nation-states, each with its own set of laws and policies. Proponents of a strong central government became known as the Federalists.

On the other side were those who wanted to avoid any chance of ever living under a repressive and tyrannical government. They fought for a system in which the power to make decisions would mostly stay with the individual states. They became known as the Anti-Federalists. Both sides in the discussion wanted what was best for their new country. But exactly what that entailed was the subject of hot debate—one that continues to this day.

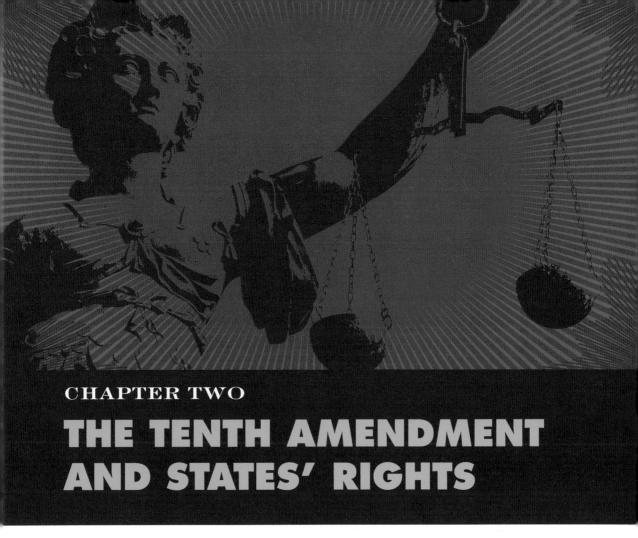

CHAPTER TWO

THE TENTH AMENDMENT AND STATES' RIGHTS

Take one look at the Bill of Rights and it is easy to see why some people fought so hard for it to be included in the Constitution. After all, these ten amendments protect the very rights long denied to American colonists under British rule and long fought for during the American Revolution. The Bill of Rights gave American citizens the right to free speech and due process. It allowed people to worship as they chose, to keep and bear arms, and to be protected from unreasonable search and seizure. These amendments laid out the rules by which people could and could not be prosecuted for crimes. They also guaranteed them the right to fair, speedy trials that would be decided by a jury of their peers, rather than by the whims and prejudices of a single judge or other authority figure.

The Tenth Amendment, however, was different from most of the other amendments in the Bill of Rights. Although it seemed somewhat simple on the surface, its vague wording is the result of the emotion, anxiety, and fierce debate that went into it. This amendment was, for many Americans, the central principle of the entire Constitution. This was because it was the one that stated what powers the federal government had and, more importantly, what powers it did not possess. The Tenth Amendment sought to express the limits of federal power, thereby identifying what rights belonged to the individual states and the people living within them.

Opposing Views

The people who felt that the federal government should have a great deal of power were known as Federalists. They were led by such historical figures as Alexander Hamilton, John Jay, and future president James Madison. They were convinced that the best government for this new nation was a strong, centralized one. Otherwise, they believed, the states would lapse into total lawlessness and chaos would reign. Their dozens of essays and letters published in various newspapers—today known collectively as the Federalist Papers—encouraged readers to accept their viewpoints. Businesspeople and bankers tended to rally behind them because the Federalists also favored the creation of a national bank and mint and sound national fiscal policies.

James Madison is often called the Father of the Constitution because he dedicated so much time and effort to the creation of the document. Even though George Washington was assigned to be the head of the Constitutional Convention, it was Madison who stepped in and led

James Madison has not received as much recognition for his role as a Founding Father as George Washington, Thomas Jefferson, and others. But it was Madison who, in many ways, helped lead the country toward a better, stronger government during the Constitutional Convention of 1787 and the drafting of the Bill of Rights in 1789.

the gathering. To Federalists like Madison, the Tenth Amendment was particularly important because it detailed just who had what powers. This reduced the likelihood of confusion between the federal and state governments and created a clear and clean division of rights and responsibilities.

Madison states in Federalist No. 45, "The powers delegated by the proposed Constitution to the federal government are few and defined. Those which are to remain in the State governments are numerous and indefinite. The former [federal powers] will be exercised principally on external objects, as war, peace, negotiation, and foreign commerce; with which last the power of taxation will, for the most part, be connected." Madison strongly believed that this division of authority was created in order "to ensure protection of our fundamental liberties." He also added, "The powers reserved to the several States will extend to all the objects which, in the ordinary course of affairs, concern the lives, liberties, and properties of the people, and the internal order, improvement, and prosperity of the State."

Given that the Constitution already created this clear division between a few important federal powers and all remaining powers delegated to the states, some Federalists did not quite understand the necessity for the Bill of Rights. Why take the time to outline in a series of amendments what the federal government could not do when it was never empowered by the Constitution to do these things in the first place? In Federalist No. 84, Hamilton wrote, "For why declare that things shall not be done which there is no power to do?" He and other Federalists also worried that the Bill of Rights could actually be dangerous. If these ten amendments that spelled out specific rights and protections were added to the Constitution, it might imply that any rights not specified would be considered unprotected or even unlawful.

Hammer v. Dagenhart

One of the most influential court cases centering on the Tenth Amendment is *Hammer v. Dagenhart* (1918). It all began with child labor. Not only did poor young children work, but they had full-time jobs in dirty and dangerous factories. In some factories, almost half of the employees were between the ages of seven and sixteen years old. These children were rarely given formal education beyond the first few years of their lives.

In the mid-1800s, child labor laws began to appear in different states in an effort to protect these young people. The federal government stayed out of the issue, allowing the individual states to address it. This was because stating how many hours a child could work or at what ages was viewed by the states as interfering with an employer's right to enter into a contract. This kind of interference—even for the good of America's children—was not a constitutional right granted to the federal government.

Concern for the welfare of American children finally began to grow, however, and people began to push for change to the states' labor laws. Two men, Edward Keating and Robert Owen, located a loophole in the law that would allow federal intervention. Using the Commerce Clause of the Constitution (see page 33), which gave the government the authority to regular interstate business, they proposed the Child Labor Act of 1916. This act would prohibit (forbid) the interstate shipment of products made by businesses that employed children who were too young or worked too many hours.

The bill passed and became law—but many people were not happy with it. Factory operators, owners of family businesses where sons and daughters helped out, and even struggling families that relied upon their children's wages for survival were all upset with the changes to the law. One North Carolina man, Roland Dagenhart, who worked in a cotton mill with his two teenaged sons, argued that the law was unconstitutional. He claimed the federal government was not empowered to tell people how to run their businesses.

The case eventually reached the Supreme Court, where the U.S. attorney for the Western District of North Carolina, W. C. Hammer, argued that the new child labor law was necessary to protect the public good. The court was divided 5–4, with the majority ruling in favor of Dagenhart. The nation's first child labor law was officially overturned.

On the other side of the issue were the Anti-Federalists, led by people such as Thomas Jefferson and Patrick Henry. They felt the Bill of Rights was an absolutely essential and necessary part of the Constitution. Jefferson believed that the Tenth Amendment was so important that he referred to it as "the foundation of the Constitution." Although these men agreed that a Constitution was needed, they deeply feared one that would grant too much power to the federal government—power that rightfully belonged to the states and the American people. "The government which governs least, governs best," stated Jefferson.

Troubled Times

The Tenth Amendment went to the heart of the Federalist/Anti-Federalist debate by attempting to identify the limits of federal power and delineate state's rights and the rights of the people. The amendment was designed to make the various layers of American government more efficient and less complicated, with fewer areas of overlap and dispute. In practice, however, it did just the opposite in many cases throughout history.

One of the first important court cases that tested the Tenth Amendment's attempted

The establishment of a federal bank angered those who felt the government had no constitutional right to establish or operate a national bank. The Second Bank of the United States (*right*) opened a branch in Baltimore, which led to the 1819 case *McCulloch v. Maryland.*

division of federal and state powers was *McCulloch v. Maryland* in 1819. At that time, the state of Maryland believed that the federal government did not have the power to establish a national bank. After all, it wasn't listed as a right in the Constitution. Despite this lack of explicit (spelled

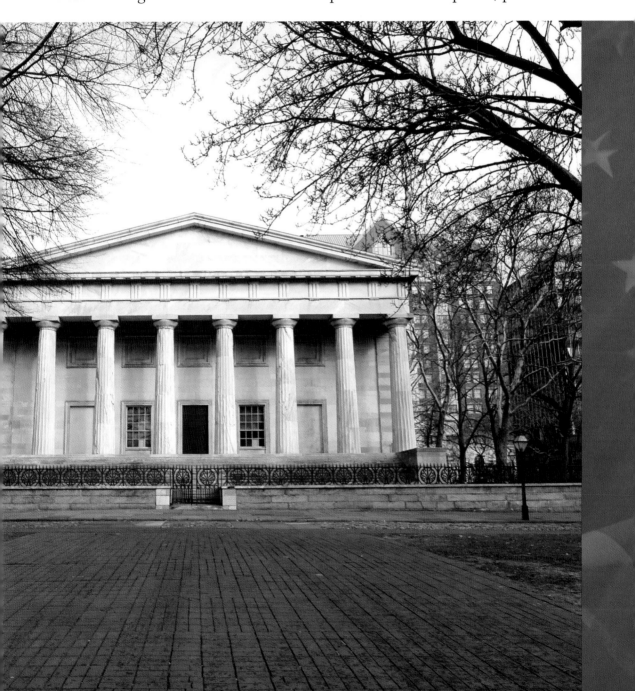

out) constitutional permission, the U.S. government had created the Second Bank of the United States. It was based in Philadelphia but also opened a branch in Baltimore, Maryland, without that state's approval. In response, Maryland taxed the bank's operations and imposed fines for nonpayment of the tax. When branch manager James McCulloch refused to pay the taxes and fines, Maryland took the bank to court.

Eventually the case went all the way to the Supreme Court. Who won? The federal government did. According to Chief Justice John Marshall, creating a national bank with branches throughout the country encouraged business between states, and that was good for the entire country. In addition, Marshall stated that Maryland could not tax a "national entity." Marshall added, "Let the end be legitimate, let it be within the scope of the Constitution, and all means which are appropriate, which are plainly adapted to that end, which are not prohibited, but consistent with the letter and spirit of the Constitution, are constitutional." What he meant was that if the ultimate goal is legitimate and constitutional—in this case, the establishment of a national bank—and all of the actions necessary to reach that goal are not in direct violation of the Constitution, then those actions must also be considered constitutional.

Why was this case so important? It was the first time the courts expressed the fact that the federal government had more powers than those few explicitly spelled out in the Constitution. In addition to its expressly stated powers, the Constitution provided the federal government with other, implied powers. The *McCulloch v. Maryland* decision also determined that states had no choice but to obey federal laws. Federal laws took precedence over state laws. This outcome was precisely what the anti-Federalists had feared—a court decision granting the federal government more power than explicitly specified in the Constitution and the ability to trump state law.

February Term 1817 — (Judgments

Henry Aston
53 —
v.
Bazaliel Wells & the
heirs and Representatives of
Arnold H. Dohrman dec'd

This cause came on to be heard on the transcript of the Record and was argued by Counsel on consideration whereof — It is decreed and ordered, that the Decree of the Circuit Court for the District of Ohio in this case be and the same is hereby affirmed with Costs — March 6th

James W. McCulloch
66 —
vs
The State of Maryland &
John James, as well for the
State as for himself

This cause came on to be heard on the transcript of the Record of the Court of Appeals of the State of Maryland, and was argued by Counsel, on consideration whereof, It is the opinion of this Court, that the act of the Legislature of Maryland entitled "An act to impose a tax on all Banks or Branches thereof in the State of Maryland not chartered by the Legislature" is contrary to the Constitution of the United States and void, and therefore that the said Court of Appeals of the State of Maryland erred in affirming the Judgment of the Baltimore County Court in which Judgment was rendered against James W. McCulloch but that the said Court of Appeals of Maryland ought to have reversed the said Judgment of the said Baltimore County Court and to have given Judgment for the said appellant McCulloch — It is therefore adjudged and ordered, that the said Judgment of the said Court of Appeals of the State of Maryland in this case be and the same is hereby reversed and annulled — and this Court proceeding to render such Judgment as the said Court of Appeals should have rendered; It is further adjudged and ordered, that the judgment of the said Baltimore County Court be reversed and annulled, and that Judgment be entered in the said Baltimore County Court for the said James W. McCulloch. —
March 6th

Chief Justice John Marshall's decision in the *McCulloch v. Maryland* case (*above*) fueled the fire of debate between those who felt the government needed to have more power and those who felt it needed less.

The Issue of Slavery

Several decades later, a national crisis developed over the issue of slavery that not only challenged the Tenth Amendment but also robbed it of its power for some time. Until the Civil War, most states preferred that the federal government allow them to make their own decisions regarding state business and local issues.

This all changed when the antislavery movement began to gather strength. As federal legislation began to chip away at slaveholders' rights, the Southern states objected. The South was heavily dependent upon slave labor to work its cash crops of cotton, tobacco, and rice.

A group of African American slaves gather on the plantation of Confederate General Thomas Drayton in South Carolina in the early 1860s. Slavery was one of the biggest issues ever to test the Tenth Amendment and its balancing of federal powers versus states' rights.

When Abraham Lincoln was elected president in 1860, the pressure to end slavery intensified. In protest, eleven Southern states seceded from the Union and formed the Confederate States of America. They believed that slavery was a state right—not a federal one. This disagreement resulted in the Civil War (1861–1865) and the creation of the Thirteenth Amendment, which abolished slavery throughout the country.

Although ending slavery was a noble goal for the nation, it came in direct conflict with the state powers provided by the Tenth Amendment. Because the Constitution failed to explicitly mention slavery and the federal government's right to regulate it, slave-holding seemed to fall under the category of states' rights guaranteed by the Tenth Amendment. For this reason, a constitutional amendment explicitly outlawing slavery in every state was required to get around this legal obstacle to federally mandated abolition.

The controversy over the Tenth Amendment was far from over, however. Again and again, the issue of state versus federal powers would rear its head in cases throughout the country. And each time, it would raise the same question all over again: where do the federal government's powers end and states' rights begin?

THE FEDERAL GOVERNMENT WINS SOME AND LOSES SOME

Much of the legal confusion and philosophical conflict that have long surrounded the Tenth Amendment is due to its ambiguous wording. A number of phrases can be interpreted very broadly—and often are. Over time, some terms used in the amendment have changed meaning. Or have they? It is often a matter of opinion more than anything else.

Although there were other court cases that challenged and explored the power of the Tenth Amendment, it was not until President Franklin D. Roosevelt created his New Deal programs during the Great Depression (1929–1941) that the amendment would undergo its greatest test. The question of exactly where the limit on

The Tenth Amendment in Action: Inside *South Dakota v. Dole* (1987)

Underage drinking is illegal and unacceptable. There is general agreement throughout society, government, and the courts about this. Yet there have been surprisingly bitter constitutional debates about what constitutes "underage" and who gets to decide what a state's legal drinking age should be.

In 1984, Congress passed legislation called the National Minimum Drinking Age Act. It stated that 5 percent of Federal Aid Highway Act money would be withheld from any state that did not adopt a minimum legal drinking age of twenty-one. This meant that a state would not receive the funds necessary to build and maintain its federal interstate highways.

This new federal rule made the legislature of South Dakota very angry. The state normally sold beer to nineteen year olds, but it could not afford to lose its federal highway funds. The state decided to sue, naming Secretary of Transportation Elizabeth Dole as defendant because it was her department that enforced this new legislation.

In *South Dakota v. Dole*, the Supreme Court ruled that Congress was allowed to set the national drinking age under the Taxing and Spending Clause because it was for the "general welfare" of American citizens. It also ruled that the act did not violate the Tenth Amendment as South Dakota claimed because states were being "pressured" to comply with it but were not absolutely required to.

those powers lay would once again be debated and decided, at least for the time being.

A Country in Need

Roosevelt was president of the United States when the nation and its people were literally struggling to survive. The depression had devastated

the country. Unemployment soared. Families stood in line for food. Businesses were closing, and banks were unstable. During Roosevelt's presidential campaign, he had made great promises: "I pledge you, I pledge myself, to a New Deal for the American people. This is more

This long line in front of a Chicago, Illinois, soup kitchen was a familiar sight during the Great Depression. The hungry and the homeless lined up to survive another day in this dark period of American history.

than a political campaign; it's a call to arms. Give me your help, not to win votes alone, but to win in this crusade to restore America to its own people." The people were desperate for leadership and change. They looked to their government for help out of this catastrophe—and, in doing so, gave it more power than it had ever had before.

Roosevelt's campaign promises of a return to work and prosperity persuaded people to elect him president, and he quickly made good on his word. He created many New Deal programs designed to put the nation's people back to work. In the process, the country's infrastructure, natural environments, and culture were improved in many ways. The New Deal included programs that still exist today, such as the Federal Communications Commission (FCC), the Federal Deposit Insurance Corporation (FDIC), the Federal Housing Administration (FHA), and the Social Security Board. During his first term, Roosevelt created work for more than five million previously unemployed people.

However, not every New Deal program was a success or even enjoyed popular, political, or legal support. Roosevelt created dozens of programs, some of which the Supreme Court declared unconstitutional. The justices argued that the president violated the Tenth Amendment by overstepping the bounds of federal executive power. The Agricultural Adjustment Act, for example, was declared unconstitutional. This New Deal program paid farmers to destroy some of their crops and livestock in order to reduce an oversupplied market and force crop prices to go back up.

Altogether almost a dozen of Roosevelt's New Deal programs were declared unconstitutional by the Supreme Court because they tried to use federal power to overrule the policies of state governments. The Supreme Court declared in these decisions that if a state had a crisis, it was to take care of it on its own, instead of relying on a federal program or other forms of assistance. Each time one of these New Deal programs was called into question, it reminded people that the wording of the Tenth Amendment was often open to interpretation and confusion.

Three Clauses

As time has passed, especially in the wake of Progressive Era regulatory reform and Roosevelt's massive New Deal program, the federal government has developed a great deal of control over areas of national scope and importance. This federal influence extends into agriculture, the manufacturing industry, and

Millions of trucks are weighed daily at highway weigh stations by Department of Transportation officials. Few truckers may think about the Tenth Amendment and the right to regulate interstate commerce that it grants to the federal government, yet this right affects every trip that drivers make.

labor unions. This power is primarily granted by three clauses found in Article 1, Section 8 of the Constitution.

The Commerce Clause has been dissected and analyzed a great deal since the Constitution's framers first wrote it. It states that "Congress

shall have power to regulate commerce with foreign nations and among the several states, and with the Indian Tribes." Some experts claim that the Constitutional Convention delegates used the word "commerce" to mean nothing more than trade. Others believe they meant it to encompass all economic activities. If the latter is true, the clause gives the government freedom to regulate almost all aspects of American business. Originally, the clause was interpreted to cover only interstate commerce (trade and commerce between two or more states). Over the years, however, federal courts have viewed it as also pertaining to intrastate commerce (trade and commerce within a single state).

Another clause that proves to be controversial and open to widely differing interpretations is the Taxing and Spending Clause. It states that "Congress shall have power to lay and collect taxes, duties, imposts [a tax or duty], and excises, to pay the debts and provide for the common Defence and general welfare of the United States; but all Duties, Imposts, and Excises shall be uniform throughout the United States." This clause has been used by the federal government, with the support of the courts, to justify federal taxes, including income taxes, payroll taxes, and tariffs (taxes on imported goods). But the clause's vague wording about "general welfare" has inspired much political debate. Even the Federalists and Anti-Federalists argued over it. Madison insisted that the clause be interpreted narrowly, while Hamilton argued for a broad understanding of it. Madison felt taxes should only be raised for specific purposes of national importance, like providing for the military or funding the regulation of interstate commerce. Hamilton felt taxes could and should be raised for more general spending purposes as long as it would benefit the entire country, rather than one state or region only.

The third clause that has raised constitutional questions concerning the division of power between federal and state governments is the Necessary and Proper Clause. It states, "Congress shall have

Gun control activists Jim and Sarah Brady (*far right*) meet with President Bill Clinton (*seated*), Vice President Al Gore, and Attorney General Janet Reno in the White House's Oval Office to sign the Brady Bill.

power to make all laws which shall be necessary and proper for carrying into Execution the foregoing powers, and all other powers vested by this Constitution in the Government of the United States, or in any Department or Office thereof." What exactly does "necessary and proper" mean? These terms are so vague that they can be interpreted to mean many different things. In fact, they are so generic that this clause is nicknamed the Elastic Clause because it can cover anything and everything. The Necessary and Proper Clause has enabled Congress to claim virtually any power for itself that its members deem appropriate. Over the years, Congress has indeed used the clause to expand its power. How far the Elastic Clause can stretch before snapping is a question that is still unknown.

Gun Rulings

Another key Tenth Amendment case occurred in 1995 with *United States v. Lopez*. For the first time in more than fifty years, the Supreme Court ruled that the federal government had acted outside its power under the Commerce Clause. In this case, a senior at a Texas high school brought a concealed handgun to school with him. He was arrested and charged with violating the Gun-Free School Zones Act of 1990. In *United States v. Lopez*, the Supreme Court decided that Congress had exceeded its constitutional authority when it passed the 1990 law prohibiting gun possession in local school zones.

A similar decision was arrived at in 1997 in *Printz v. United States*. Four years earlier, President Bill Clinton had signed into law the Brady Handgun Violence Prevention Act, also known as the Brady Bill. It required that federal background checks be made on anyone purchasing a firearm in the United States. This way, Congress hoped, guns would not be sold to people who were considered a threat to public safety

People's simmering emotions often come to the surface when arguing about issues like taxes and money. During protests like this Taxpayer March in Washington, D.C., citizens vent their frustration with the federal government and its policies.

(convicted felons, fugitives from justice, unlawful aliens, etc.). The act was named for James Brady, the White House press secretary who was shot during John Hinckley Jr.'s attempted assassination of President Ronald Reagan in 1981.

Although the bill was signed into law in 1993, it was not slated to take effect until the end of 1998. In the meantime, a number of additional provisions were put into place. These included requiring firearms dealers to track transfers of handguns and then send notification of the transfers to the locality's chief law enforcement officer. These officers, in turn, had five days to conduct thorough background checks on the gun purchasers.

Two chief law enforcement officers filed lawsuits that challenged the constitutionality of these interim provisions. They felt it was wrong to use congressional action to force local authorities—rather than federal authorities—to carry out federal law. In the end, a majority of Supreme Court justices ruled that these provisions were indeed unconstitutional. Background checks conducted by local and state law enforcement became optional, while the Federal Bureau of Investigation (FBI) conducted the bulk of the checks.

It is clear from the Supreme Court's difficulty in maintaining a consistent position on the boundaries of federal power enshrined in the Tenth Amendment that federal powers versus states' rights is a very complicated question. Over the years, the question has not gotten any easier to answer. Although the specific issues change, the dilemma of striking a fair balance between federal powers and states' rights remains the same.

CHAPTER FOUR

FEDERALISM AND STATES' RIGHTS TODAY

If the framers of the Constitution had realized that hundreds of years later people would still be arguing over the interpretation of the document and its amendments, would they have written it differently? There is no way to know the answer, but chances are they might have spent a little more time clarifying and spelling out any overly vague terms. Of course, the Constitutional Convention delegates could never have imagined how the United States and its people would change over the centuries. Neither could they have anticipated how historical developments would alter the effect of older laws and make necessary new ones to account for changing times and conditions.

Today, the Tenth Amendment continues to be one of the parts of the Constitution that inspires the most controversy and debate. Contemporary issues like gun ownership, health care, environmental standards, the death penalty, medical marijuana, same-sex marriage, and assisted suicide all hinge upon the Constitution's division between federal powers and states' rights. The tense push-pull between the federal government and the states continues as each side tries to establish, defend, and expand its authority. The effects of this ongoing conflict are felt everywhere—including the classroom.

A Return to State Sovereignty?

As of early 2010, thirty-eight states in this country have introduced "state sovereignty resolutions" asserting their power under the Tenth Amendment. Tired of the federal government's involvement in too many issues they consider to be state or local matters, these states have gone on the offensive to fight for greater states' rights. Utah State Representative Carl Wimmer told FOX News, "This has been boiling for years, and it's finally come to a head." Georgia State Senator Chip Pearson agrees, recently stating to FOX that "the balance of power between the states and the federal government is way out of whack ... Everything you do from the moment you wake up until you get to bed, there is some federal law or restriction." A Montana law professor who has been involved with the state sovereignty movement for more than a decade told FOX, "If the states are serious about returning the federal government to its historical origins, they're going to have to do more than pass resolutions. They're going to have to turn down [federal] money and litigate."

These amendment resolutions do not have the power of law behind them. Yet they are a clear statement to the federal government that a growing number of states and individuals are angry and demand change in the form of greater state and local power and individual rights and freedoms, especially the freedom from federal interference.

No Child Left Behind/Race to the Top

In 2002, the No Child Left Behind Act (NCLB) was passed by President George W. Bush. The act promised education funding to states, but the money came with strings attached. NCLB mandated that federal funding for education would be given only to those states that developed and administered a basic skills test for students in specific grades. States whose students did not score high enough would lose funding. Those whose students excelled would receive more money. This policy was designed to ensure that educators were teaching the necessary skills and subjects in their classrooms and their students were learning them adequately.

Is the right to determine and enforce education standards and policy for the entire nation one of the powers granted to the federal govern- ment by the Constitution? Nowhere in that document is education mentioned as an area in which the federal government can exercise policy control over the states. Because education is not mentioned specifically as a federal power, the right to determine education policy should fall to the states, according to the Tenth Amendment.

While some state departments of education objected to NCLB on the basis of its unconstitutionality, still others complained about the high cost of developing and administering the tests. Although federal funding was provided to help pay for these costs, it did not begin to cover the total bill. "The extent of the opposition to NCLB legislation is unprecedented in its scope and depth . . . While many of the resolutions protesting NCLB were symbolic, the number of states passing or intro- ducing them, as well as the number of Republican states that opposed the legislation, sent a powerful political message to Washington," states an article from the Texas Conservative Coalition.

Bruce Hunter, spokesperson for the American Federation of Teachers, applauds the intentions of the bill, yet still believes it to be unconstitutional. "Education is a state and local matter," he explains in an interview with *Education World*. "This enlarged the federal

President Barack Obama stops by the Viers Mill Elementary School in Silver Spring, Maryland, to congratulate the students for making it a National Title I No Child Left Behind Blue Ribbon school.

government's role to one that is unneeded and unnecessary . . . At some point, you give up something precious if you let the federal government tell the states and local government how to assess schools."

In 2009, NCLB was superseded (replaced) by President Barack Obama's Race to the Top (RTTT) program. This is a stimulus-based grant program in which the president has promised $4.35 billion in grant money to schools that meet certain educational standards. While the money would be appreciated by all school systems, in order to get it, they would have to teach only what the U.S. Department of Education deemed fit. Many people, from principals and city council members to parents and students, felt this was an example of the federal government intruding in areas better left to state and local policy makers. In an editorial posted on the Web site of the Tenth Amendment Center (an organization dedicated to promoting strictly limited government), Derek Sheriff wrote, "The question we should ask ourselves is, 'Do we really want the government in far-off Washington, D.C., deciding the subjects and content of our children's daily school lesson plans and how much time they spend in school?'"

Real ID

Another Tenth Amendment–related issue that has emerged in recent years is national identification cards (IDs). For identification purposes (to prove one's identity, for example), most people either carry a photo ID card, a driver's license, or a passport. However, personal identification became far more important and complicated after the terrorist attacks of September 11, 2001. Suddenly, the focus of the entire world shifted to security, safe borders, and immigration control to prevent any further incidents of violence committed by terrorists traveling freely throughout the world and within the United States.

In 2005, the Real ID Act was passed by Congress. It stated that the various identification cards issued by the fifty states had to include the same information. In addition, that information should be included in a national database in case it had to be accessed by federal law enforcement authorities. According to the Department of Homeland Security, this act would also allow additional changes to ID cards in the future. This could include the addition of biometric data such as fingerprints, retinal scans, and DNA information.

Identification cards have become more high-tech and vital to national security in recent years. Proposed programs like Real ID would further this trend.

A number of political groups and states spoke out against this new national ID card system. They feared that it would be extremely difficult to administer and would threaten individual privacy. As Utah's resolution against Real IDs states, the act was "in opposition to the

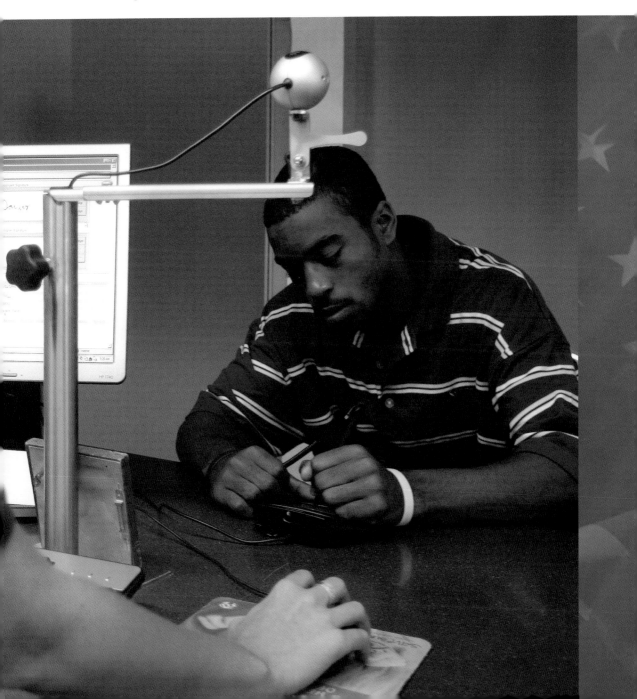

Jeffersonian principles of individual liberty, free markets, and limited government." Following the act's passage, more than three dozen states passed legislation opposing it.

Without one of these federally mandated identification cards, Americans may find themselves unable to board an airplane, get their Social Security checks, open a bank account, or even get a job. Anthony Romero, executive director of the American Civil Liberties Union, says that "Real ID is an unfunded mandate that violates the Constitution's Tenth Amendment on state powers, destroys' states dual sovereignty [division of powers between state and federal governments], and consolidates every American's private information, leaving all of us far more vulnerable to identity thieves" (as quoted by Anthony Romero).

Gun Manufacturing and Monitoring

The right to bear arms is enshrined by the Second Amendment to the U.S. Constitution. However, who can and can't own a gun, what kind of gun they can own, and how and when they can buy a gun are complicated and unresolved questions. The Brady Bill and other gun

Buying and owning a gun is one of an American's basic constitutional rights. Over the years, however, the government has put a number of rules in place creating restrictions on who can buy guns, where and when they can buy guns, and what kinds of guns they can buy.

control legislation has put limits on gun ownership as well as on interstate weapons commerce.

In late 2009, the state of Montana signed a new law that stated in
part that "a personal firearm, a firearm accessory, or ammunition that is

manufactured commercially or privately in Montana and that remains within the borders of Montana is not subject to federal law or federal regulation, including registration, under the authority of Congress to regulate interstate commerce." In other words, any gun made entirely within the state and kept within the state would not be required to be registered by a gun buyer. Nor would gun sellers be required to run background checks on buyers of Montana-manufactured guns or keep records of the sales of these guns. The federal Bureau of Alcohol, Tobacco, Firearms, and Explosives (ATF) told Montana that all federal gun regulations continue to apply, despite the passage of this state law.

Gary Marbut, who is president of the Montana Shooting Sports Association, said in response, "We feel very strongly that the federal government has gone way too far in attempting to regulate a lot of activity that occurs only in-state. It's time for Montana and her sister states to take a stand against the bullying federal government, which the legislature and governor have done and we are doing with this lawsuit." Other states followed Montana's example, including Texas, Arkansas, South Carolina, and Florida.

Future Issues

Other cases hinging upon the question of federal versus states' rights pop up across the country regularly, and most likely will keep doing so. Some of the issues being reviewed by federal courts today include same-sex marriage, medical marijuana, environmental standards and requirements, the death penalty, and assisted suicide. Each one of these topics is controversial. Passionate debate on these issues ranges from what should and should not be legal to who gets to decide the answer in the first place—the federal government or the individual states.

The Tenth Amendment is not only about federal powers and states' rights. It's also about the individual citizen's rights. On the steps of the Supreme Court in Washington, D.C., demonstrators hold signs in support of Oregon's physician-assisted suicide law.

When the framers of the Constitution drafted this history-changing document more than two hundred years ago, they had no way of foreseeing how society and its most pressing issues would evolve. They did, however, know how important independence, autonomy (self-government), and individual rights were to all human beings. As the battle over the power and scope of the federal government versus what rights belong to the states and their residents rages on, it might benefit both sides to stop and ask themselves one question: what would the Constitution's framers—Thomas Jefferson, Alexander Hamilton, James Madison, John Jay, and others—have advised?

AMENDMENTS TO THE U.S. CONSTITUTION

First Amendment (proposed 1789; ratified 1791): Freedom of religion, speech, press, assembly, and petition

Second Amendment (proposed 1789; ratified 1791): Right to bear arms

Third Amendment (proposed 1789; ratified 1791): No quartering of soldiers in private houses in times of peace

Fourth Amendment (proposed 1789; ratified 1791): Interdiction of unreasonable search and seizure; requirement of search warrants

Fifth Amendment (proposed 1789; ratified 1791): Indictments; due process; self-incrimination; double jeopardy; eminent domain

Sixth Amendment (proposed 1789; ratified 1791): Right to a fair and speedy public trial; notice of accusations; confronting one's accuser; subpoenas; right to counsel

Seventh Amendment (proposed 1789; ratified 1791): Right to a trial by jury in civil cases

Eighth Amendment (proposed 1789; ratified 1791): No excessive bail and fines; no cruel or unusual punishment

Ninth Amendment (proposed 1789; ratified 1791): Protection of unenumerated rights (rights inferred from other legal rights but that are not themselves coded or enumerated in written constitution and laws)

Tenth Amendment (proposed 1789; ratified 1791): Limits the power of the federal government

Eleventh Amendment (proposed 1794; ratified 1795): Sovereign immunity (immunity of states from suits brought by out-of-state citizens and foreigners living outside of states' borders)

Twelfth Amendment (proposed 1803; ratified 1804): Revision of presidential election procedures (electoral college)

Thirteenth Amendment (proposed 1865; ratified 1865): Abolition of slavery

Fourteenth Amendment (proposed 1866; ratified 1868): Citizenship; state due process; application of Bill of Rights to states; revision to apportionment of congressional representatives; denies public office to anyone who has rebelled against the United States

Fifteenth Amendment (proposed 1869; ratified 1870): Suffrage no longer restricted by race

Sixteenth Amendment (proposed 1909; ratified 1913): Allows federal income tax

Seventeenth Amendment (proposed 1912; ratified 1913): Direct election to the U.S. Senate by popular vote

Eighteenth Amendment (proposed 1917; ratified 1919): Prohibition of alcohol

Nineteenth Amendment (proposed 1919; ratified 1920): Women's suffrage

Twentieth Amendment (proposed 1932; ratified 1933): Term commencement for Congress (January 3) and president (January 20)

Twenty-first Amendment (proposed 1933; ratified 1933): Repeal of Eighteenth Amendment (Prohibition)

Twenty-second Amendment (proposed 1947; ratified 1951): Limits president to two terms

Twenty-third Amendment (proposed 1960; ratified 1961): Representation of District of Columbia in electoral college

Twenty-fourth Amendment (proposed 1962; ratified 1964): Prohibition of restriction of voting rights due to nonpayment of poll taxes

Twenty-fifth Amendment (proposed 1965; ratified 1967): Presidential succession

Twenty-sixth Amendment (proposed 1971; ratified 1971): Voting age of eighteen

Twenty-seventh Amendment (proposed 1789; ratified 1992): Congressional compensation

Proposed but Unratified Amendments

Congressional Apportionment Amendment (proposed 1789; still technically pending): Apportionment of U.S. representatives

Titles of Nobility Amendment (proposed 1810; still technically pending): Prohibition of titles of nobility

Corwin Amendment (proposed 1861; still technically pending though superseded by Thirteenth Amendment): Preservation of slavery

Child Labor Amendment (proposed 1924; still technically pending): Congressional power to regulate child labor

Equal Rights Amendment (proposed 1972; expired): Prohibition of inequality of men and women

District of Columbia Voting Rights Amendment (proposed 1978; expired): District of Columbia voting rights

GLOSSARY

amendment A change or addition made to a legal document.

anarchy A state of society in which there is no government or law.

Anti-Federalists Opponents of federalism, or a strong central government.

Articles The main body of the U.S. Constitution. Following the Preamble (introduction), the Constitution has seven Articles addressing legislative power, executive power, judicial power, states' powers and limits, the amendment process, federal power, and the ratification process.

Bill of Rights The first ten amendments to the U.S. Constitution that more clearly outline the various rights and powers of the federal government, the states, and the individual citizen.

biometric Describing technology that allows for the recognition and identification of individuals based on physical or behavioral traits, such as fingerprints; DNA; face, retina, and iris recognition; gait; and voice.

delegate A person authorized or sent to speak and act for others; a representative at a convention.

dictatorship A country, government, or form of government in which absolute power is held by a dictator, or supreme leader.

due process Fair treatment under the law.

Federalists Advocates of federalism, or a strong central government, including a strong central bank that would establish sound national fiscal policies.

interpret To explain the meaning of; to make understandable; to bring out the meaning of; to give one's own conception of something.

interstate business Commerce between states within a country.

preamble An introductory statement, preface, or introduction.

ratify To confirm by expressing consent, approval, or formal sanction.

republic A state in which the head of government is not a monarch or other hereditary head of state. Instead the people of the nation choose their leaders and have some role or representation or say in their government.

secede To withdraw formally from an alliance, federation, or association.

tyrant A sovereign or other ruler who uses power oppressively or unjustly.

unconstitutional In violation of the U.S. Constitution; unauthorized by or inconsistent with the Constitution.

vague Not clearly, precisely, or definitely expressed or stated; indefinite in shape, form, or character; hazily or indistinctly seen or sensed; not sharp, certain, or precise in thought, feeling, or expression; not precisely determined or known; uncertain.

FOR MORE INFORMATION

American Bar Association
321 North Clark Street
Chicago, IL 60654-7598
(312) 988-5000
Web site: http://www.abanet.org
The American Bar Association is the national representative of the legal profession. Its mission is to serve equally its members (lawyers and judges) and the public by defending liberty and delivering justice.

American Law Institute
4025 Chestnut Street
Philadelphia, PA 19104
(215) 243-1600
Web site: http://www.ali.org
The American Law Institute is one of the leading independent legal organizations in the United States. It produces scholarly work to clarify, modernize, and otherwise improve the law. The institute (made up of four thousand highly accomplished and respected lawyers, judges, and law professors) drafts, discusses, revises, and publishes Restatements of the Law, model statutes, and principles of law that exert a strong influence on courts and legislatures, legal scholarship, and legal education.

Harvard Law Review
Gannett House
1511 Massachusetts Avenue
Cambridge, MA 02138
(617) 495-7889

Web site: http://www.harvardlawreview.org/index.php
The *Harvard Law Review* is an important academic forum for legal scholarship. It is designed to be an effective research tool for practicing lawyers and students of the law. The *Review* features articles by professors, judges, and lawyers, and solicits reviews of important recent books from recognized experts.

National Archives and Records Administration
8601 Adelphi Road
College Park, MD 20740-6001
1 (866) 272-6272
Web site: http://www.archives.gov
The National Archives and Records Administration is the nation's record keeper. It houses the Declaration of Independence, the Articles of Confederation, the Constitution, the Bill of Rights, the Emancipation Proclamation, and the Louisiana Purchase agreement along with other documents of national importance, like military and immigration records and even the *Apollo 11* flight plan. Archives locations in fourteen cities, from coast to coast, protect and provide public access to millions of records.

Supreme Court of the United States
1 First Street NE
Washington, DC 20543
(202) 479-3000
Web site: http://www.supremecourt.gov
The Supreme Court is the highest judicial body in the United States and leads the federal judiciary. It consists of the chief justice of the United States and eight associate justices who are nominated by the president and confirmed by a majority vote of the Senate. Once appointed, justices can serve for life. Their time on the Court ends only upon death, resignation, retirement, or conviction on impeachment charges. The Court meets in Washington, D.C., in the U.S. Supreme Court Building. The Supreme Court primarily hears appeals of lower court decisions.

Tenth Amendment Center

123 South Figueroa Street, Suite 1614

Los Angeles, CA 90012

Web site: http://www.tenthamendmentcenter.com

The Tenth Amendment Center is a national think tank that works to preserve and protect the principles of strictly limited government through information, education, and activism. The center serves as a forum for the study and exploration of state and individual sovereignty issues, focusing primarily on the decentralization of federal government power.

10th Amendment Foundation, Inc.

P.O. Box 1354

Abingdon, VA 24212

Web site: http://www.10thamendmentfoundation.org

This group describes itself as "a grass roots, non-partisan, non-profit, political, educational corporation." According to its Web site, it was created by U.S. citizens who are "upset with the run-away violations of the Rule of Law who want to find ways to restrain the Federal Government from exceeding the limited powers granted to it by the people" through the Constitution.

Web Sites

Due to the changing nature of Internet links, Rosen Publishing has developed an online list of Web sites related to the subject of this book. This site is updated regularly. Please use this link to access the list:

http://www.rosenlinks.com/ausc/10th

FOR FURTHER READING

Arnheim, Michael. *U.S. Constitution for Dummies*. Hoboken, NJ: Wiley Publishing, 2009.

Ball, Lea. *The Federalist–Anti-Federalist Debate Over States' Rights*. New York, NY: Rosen Publishing Group, 2005.

Burgan, Michael. *The Creation of the U.S. Constitution* (Graphic History). Mankato, MN: Capstone Press, 2007.

Cheney, Lynn, and Greg Harlin. *We the People: The Story of Our Constitution*. New York, NY: Simon & Schuster Children's Publishing, 2008.

Finkelman, Paul. *American Documents: The Constitution*. Des Moines, IA: National Geographic Children's Books, 2005.

Fradin, Dennis Brindell. *The Bill of Rights* (Turning Points in U.S. History). Tarrytown, NY: Marshall Cavendish Children's Books, 2008.

Fradin, Dennis Brindell. *The Founders: The 39 Stories Behind the U.S. Constitution*. New York, NY: Walker Books for Young Readers, 2005.

Isaacs, Sally Senzell. *Understanding the Bill of Rights* (Documenting Early America). New York, NY: Crabtree Publishing Co., 2008.

Isaacs, Sally Senzell. *Understanding the U.S. Constitution* (Documenting Early America). New York, NY: Crabtree Publishing Co., 2008.

JusticeLearning.org. *The United States Constitution: What It Says, What It Means: A Hip Pocket Guide*. New York, NY: Oxford University Press, 2005.

Leavitt, Amie J. *The Bill of Rights in Translation: What It Really Means*. Mankato, MN: Capstone Press, 2008.

Maestro, Betsy. *A New Nation: The United States 1783–1815*. New York, NY: Collins, 2009.

Ransom, Candice F. *Who Wrote the U.S. Constitution and Other Questions About the Constitutional Convention of 1787*. Minneapolis, MN: Lerner Classroom, 2010.

Roberts, Russell. *Alexander Hamilton* (Profiles in American History). Hockessin, DE: Mitchell Lane Publishers, 2006.

Smith, Rich. *How Amendments Are Adopted*. Edina, MN: ABDO and Daughters, 2007.

Smith, Rich. *Ninth and Tenth Amendments: The Right to More Rights*. Edina, MN: ABDO and Daughters, 2007.

Sobel, Syl. *The Bill of Rights: Protecting Our Freedom Then and Now*. Hauppauge, NY: Barron's Educational Series, 2008.

Taylor-Butler, Christine. *The Bill of Rights* (True Books). New York, NY: Children's Press, 2008.

Taylor-Butler, Christine. *The Constitution of the United States* (True Books). New York, NY: Children's Press, 2008.

Taylor-Butler, Christine. *The Supreme Court* (True Books). New York, NY: Children's Press, 2008.

Travis, Cathy. *The Constitution Translated for Kids*. Austin, TX: Ovation Books, 2008.

Yero, Judith Lloyd. *American Documents: The Bill of Rights*. Des Moines, IA: National Geographic Children's Books, 2006.

BIBLIOGRAPHY

Arnheim, Michael. *U.S. Constitution for Dummies*. Hoboken, NJ: Wiley Publishing, 2009.

Delisio, Ellen. "No Child Left Behind: What It Means to You." *Education World*, June 24, 2002. Retrieved May 2010 (http://www.educationworld.com/a_issues/issues273.shtml).

FOX News. "Health Care Bill Could Face String of Legal Challenges." December 22, 2009. Retrieved May 2010 (http://www.foxnews.com/politics/2009/12/22/health-care-face-string-legal-challenges).

Horn, Geoffrey. *The Bill of Rights and Other Amendments*. New York, NY: World Almanac Publishing, 2004.

Lively, Donald. *Landmark Supreme Court Cases*. Santa Barbara, CA: Greenwood Press, 1999.

McCullagh, Declan. "Gun Rights Groups Plan State by State Revolt." CBSNews.com, June 16, 2009. Retrieved May 2010 (http://www.cbsnews.com/8301-503544_162-5090952-503544.html).

McCullagh, Declan. "Montana Gun Suit Challenges Federal Authority." CBSNews.com, October 1, 2009. Retrieved May 2010 (http://www.cbsnews.com/8301-504383_162-5356494-504383.html).

Newman, Alex. "Lawmakers Launch 10th Amendment Task Force." *New American*, May 11, 2010. Retrieved May 2010 (http://www.thenewamerican.com/index.php/usnews/constitution/3519-lawmakers-launch-10th-amendment-task-force).

Newman, Roger K., ed. *The Constitution and Its Amendments*. Vol. 3. New York, NY: Macmillan Reference, 1999.

Romero, Anthony. "Opposing View: Repeal Real ID." *USA Today*, March 6, 2007. Retrieved May 2010 (http://www.usatoday.com/news/opinion/2007-03-05-opposing-view_N.htm).

Sheriff, Derek. "Race to the Top Is Fixed: Just Say No!" Tenth Amendment Center, January 20, 2010. Retrieved May 2010 (http://www.tenthamendmentcenter.com/2010/01/20/race-to-the-top-is-fixed-just-say-no).

Texas Conservative Coalition. "The Tenth Amendment and the Federal Government." TXCC.org. Retrieved May 2010 (http://www.txcc.org/files/TenthAmendmentIssueBrief.pdf).

Utah State Legislature. "Resolution Opposing Real ID Act." Retrieved May 2010 (http://le.utah.gov/~2007/bills/hbillenr/hr0002.htm).

Woods, Thomas, and Kevin Gutzman. *Who Killed the Constitution? The Federal Government vs. American Liberty from World War I to Barack Obama*. New York, NY: Three Rivers Press, 2009.

INDEX

A

American Revolution, 7, 9, 17
Anti-Federalists, 13, 17, 22, 24, 34
Articles of Confederation, 10–12

B

Bill of Rights, drafting of, 14–16
Bush, George W., 41

C

Civil War, 26, 27
Commerce Clause, 21, 33–34, 36
Constitutional Convention, 12, 16,
    18–20, 34, 39

E

environmental regulation, 40, 48

F

Federalist Papers, 13, 18, 20
Federalists, 13, 16, 18, 22, 34

G

Great Depression, 28, 29–32
guns, and the tenth amendment, 36–38,
    40, 46–48

H

Hamilton, Alexander, 13, 18, 20, 34, 50
Hammer v. Dagenhart, 21

health care reform bill, 4–6
Henry, Patrick, 22

J

Jay, John, 13, 18, 50
Jefferson, Thomas, 22, 46, 50

M

Madison, James, 13, 18–20, 34, 50
McCulloch v. Maryland, 23–24
medical marijuana, 40, 48

N

National Minimum Age Drinking Act, 29
Necessary and Proper Clause, 34–36
New Deal, 28, 30–32
No Child Left Behind Act (NCLB), 41–43

O

Obama, Barack, 4–6, 43

P

Printz v. United States, 36–38

R

Race to the Top, 43
Real ID, 44–46
Roosevelt, Franklin D., 28, 29–32

S

same-sex marriage, 40, 48
slavery, 16, 26–27

About the Author

Tamra Orr is the author of numerous nonfiction books for middle school and high school readers, many of them focusing on American government, history, politics, and law. She lives in the Pacific Northwest with her four children, one husband, one cat, and one dog. In her family life, Orr, much like the Supreme Court justices charged with judging the competing claims of federal powers and states' rights, struggles to strike the right balance between the powers granted to parents and the rights accorded to their children.

Photo Credits

Cover (left) Karen Bleier/AFP/Getty Images; cover (middle) Tom Williams/Roll Call/Getty Images; cover (right) Spencer Platt/Getty Images; p. 1 (top) © www.istockphoto.com/Tom Nulens; p. 1 (bottom) © www.istockphoto.com/Lee Pettet; p. 3 © www.istockphoto.com/Nic Taylor; pp. 4–5, 42–43 Chip Somodevilla/Getty Images; pp. 8, 17, 28, 39 © www.istockphoto.com/arturbo; pp. 10–11 Comstock/Getty Images; pp. 13, 26 Library of Congress Prints and Photographs Division; pp. 14–15 Alex Wong/Getty Images; p. 19 SuperStock/Getty Images; pp. 22–23 Hemera/Thinkstock; p. 25 www.ourdocuments.gov; pp. 30–31 Rolls Press/Popperfoto/Getty Images; pp. 32–33 Scott J. Ferrell/Congressional Quarterly/Getty Images; p. 35 Dirck Halstead/Time & Life Pictures/Getty Images; p. 37 Bill Clark/Roll Call/Getty Images; pp. 44–45 © AP Images; pp. 46-47 Gabriel Bouys/AFP/Getty Images; p. 49 Jay Maillin/Bloomberg/Getty Images.

Photo Researcher: Amy Feinberg